Sally

Lehrwerk für den
Englischunterricht ab Klasse 1

Activity Book 1

Erarbeitet von
Jasmin Brune
Daniela Elsner
Barbara Gleich
Stefanie Gleixner-Weyrauch
Simone Gutwerk
Marion Lugauer
Sabine Schwarz

Unter Beratung von
Jane Brockmann-Fairchild

Illustriert von
Barbara Jung, Wilfried Poll und
Gisela Vogel

Oldenbourg Schulbuchverlag, München

Draw lines. / Circle. Number. / Write.

 Say. / Tell. / Act out.

 Colour. / Draw.

 Sing.

 Cut.

 Play the game.

 Stick.

 Sally's task

 Point.

 Listen.

 Lied/Reim auf Schüler-CD und Lehrer-CD

 Geschichte/Hörtext nur auf Lehrer-CD

Redaktion: Salomé Dick, Berlin
Illustrationen: Barbara Jung, Wilfried Poll und Gisela Vogel
Umschlagkonzept: Mendell & Oberer, München
Umschlagillustration: Barbara Jung
Layout: Lisa Neuhalfen, Berlin
Technische Umsetzung: Lisa Neuhalfen, Berlin

Tonaufnahmen: FLOEDL Audioproduktion, Ziemetshausen; Thomas Blendinger, Sommerhausen

www.cornelsen.de

1. Auflage, 7. Druck 2023

Alle Drucke dieser Auflage sind inhaltlich unverändert
und können im Unterricht nebeneinander verwendet werden.

© 2015 Cornelsen Schulverlag GmbH, Berlin
© 2016 Cornelsen Verlag GmbH, Berlin

Druck: Athesiadruck GmbH

ISBN 978-3-637-01962-1

PEFC
PEFC/18-31-166 www.pefc.de

PEFC-zertifiziert
Dieses Produkt
stammt aus
nachhaltig
bewirtschafteten
Wäldern

1 🖌 Draw.

2 💬 Say your name.

1 ✏ Colour.

2 👂 💬 Listen and act out the rhyme.

1 Listen and point.

2 Listen and tick or number.

3  Draw.

4 Sing.

Sally 1 Activity Book © 2015 Cornelsen Schulverlage GmbH, Berlin

1  Listen and colour.

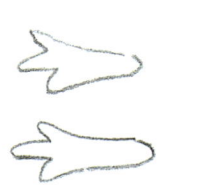

1  Listen and point.

2 🖌 Colour.

3 💬 Tell.

Sally 1 Activity Book © 2015 Cornelsen Schulverlage GmbH, Berlin

1 👂 🖌 Listen and colour.

2 💬 Tell.

1 👂 🖌 Listen and draw.

2 💬 Say the rhyme.

Sally 1 Activity Book © 2015 Cornelsen Schulverlage GmbH, Berlin

1 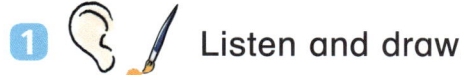 Listen and draw.

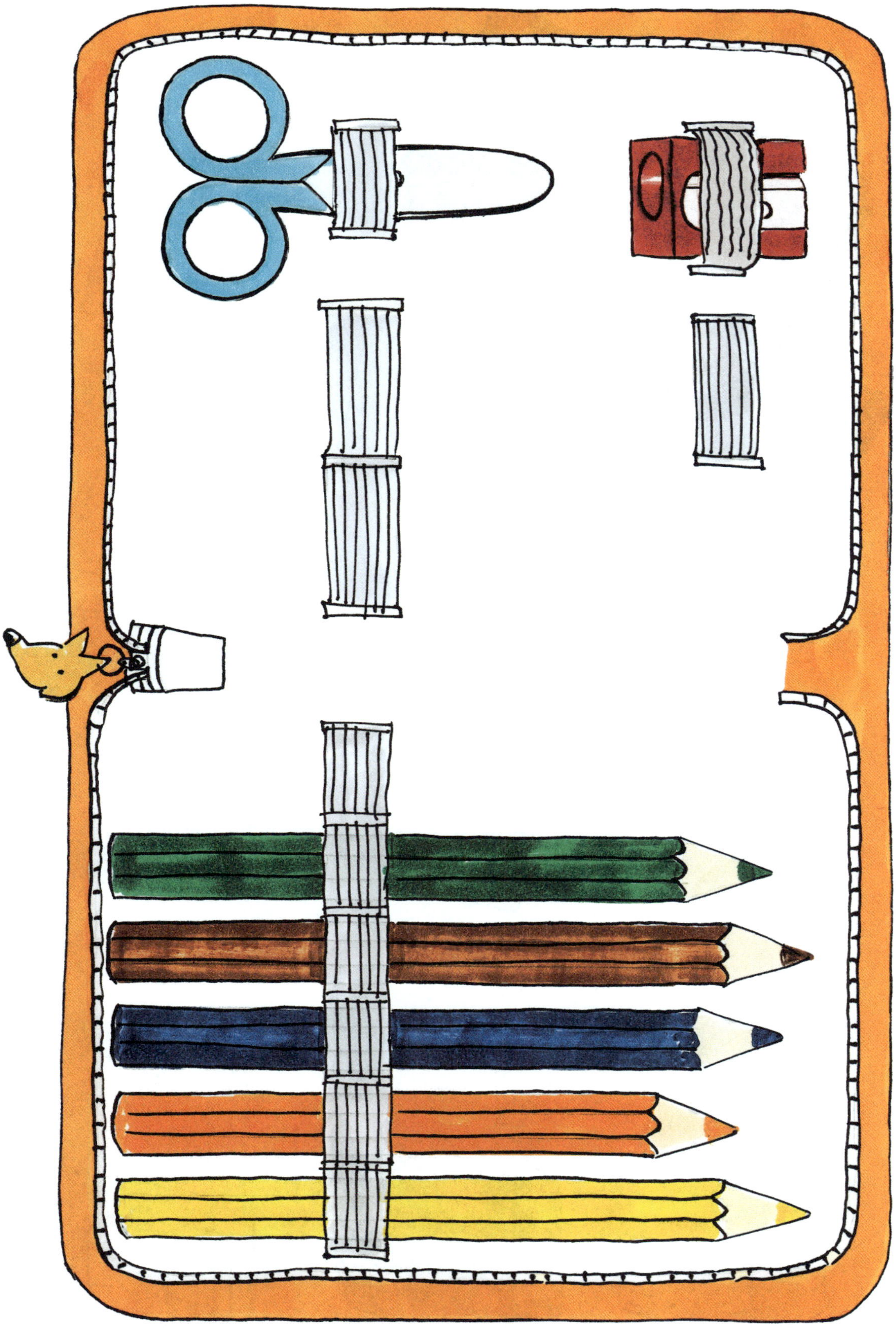

2 💬 Tell.

Sally 1 Activity Book © 2015 Cornelsen Schulverlage GmbH, Berlin

1  Listen and draw lines.

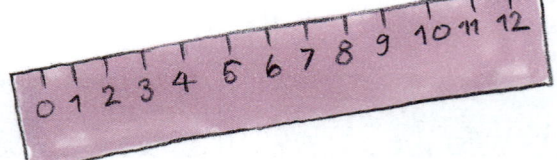

2 Tell.

Sally 1 Activity Book © 2015 Cornelsen Schulverlage GmbH, Berlin

1  Circle.

2 Tell.

Sally 1 Activity Book © 2015 Cornelsen Schulverlage GmbH, Berlin

13

1 🖌 Draw.

2 💬 Tell.

Sally 1 Activity Book © 2015 Cornelsen Schulverlage GmbH, Berlin

1  Listen and draw lines.

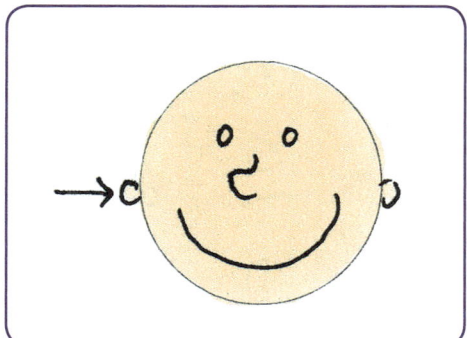

2  Say the rhyme.

Satly 1 Activity Book © 2015 Cornelsen Schulverlage GmbH, Berlin

Body and feelings

1 🖌 Colour.

2 ✏️ Count and write.

3 💬 Tell.

Sally 1 Activity Book © 2015 Cornelsen Schulverlage GmbH, Berlin

1  Colour.

2 Tell.

Sally 1 Activity Book © 2015 Cornelsen Schulverlage GmbH, Berlin

17

1 Listen and colour.

2 Draw.

3 Tell.

Sally 1 Activity Book © 2015 Cornelsen Schulverlage GmbH, Berlin

1 🖌 Colour. **2** 🎲 Play the game.

7

4

9

5

1  Listen and stick in.

2 ◯ Tell.

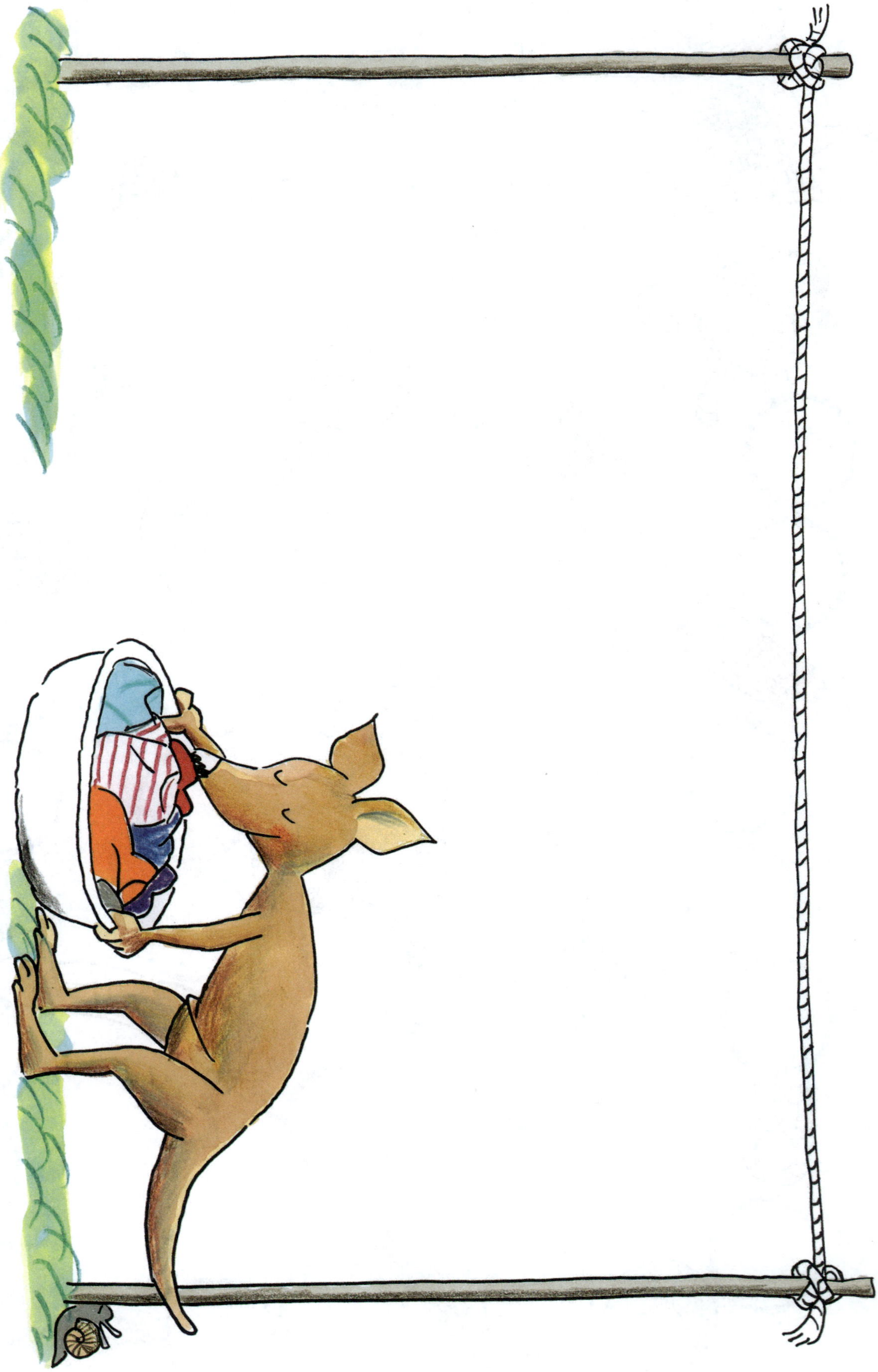

1  Listen and draw lines.

2 Tell.

3 Colour.

 **Clothes**

1 Draw your perfect outfit. Present.

Sally 1 Activity Book © 2015 Cornelsen Schulverlage GmbH, Berlin

1 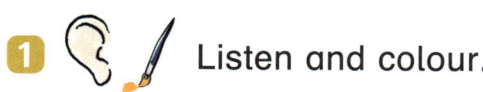 Listen and colour.

2 Sing.

Sally 1 Activity Book © 2015 Cornelsen Schulverlage GmbH, Berlin

1 ✏️ Draw a line.

Satly 1 Activity Book © 2015 Cornelsen Schulverlage GmbH, Berlin

1 Make your own animal quiz. Present.

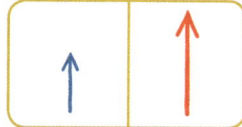 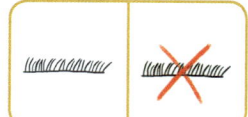

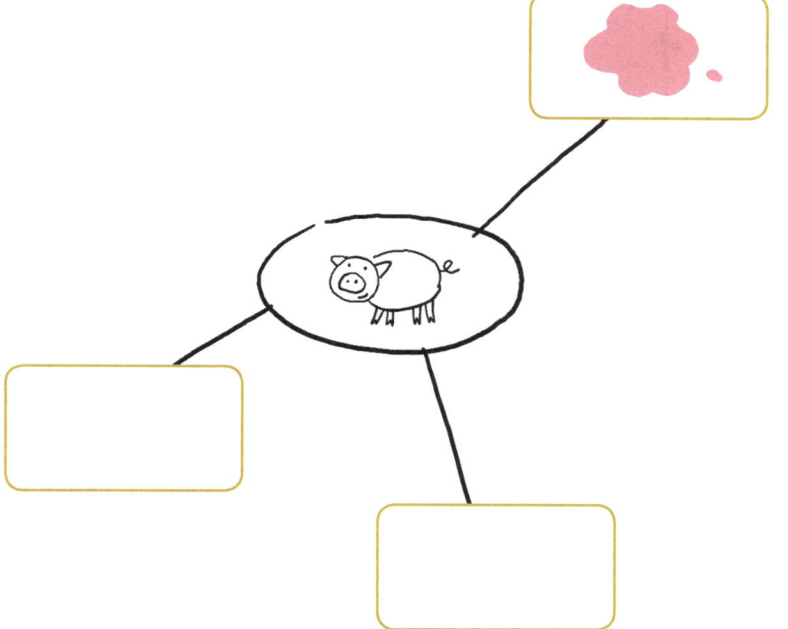

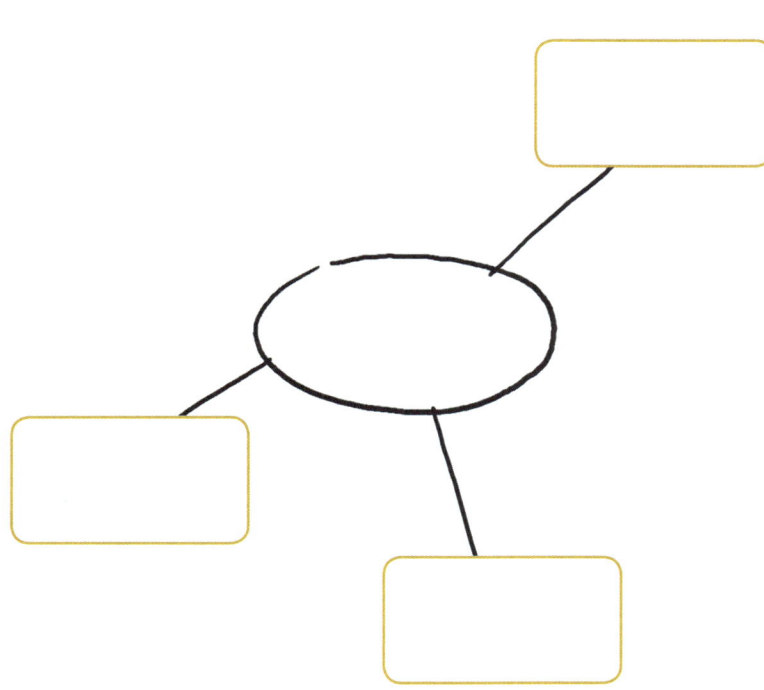

1 ✏️ Draw lines.

2 🖌️ Colour.

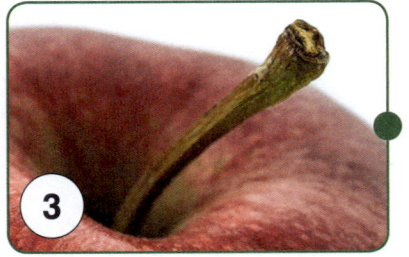

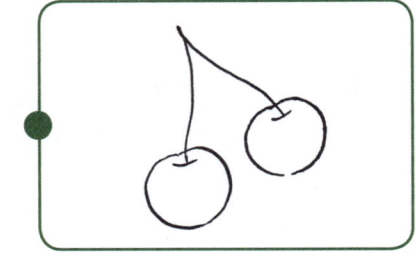

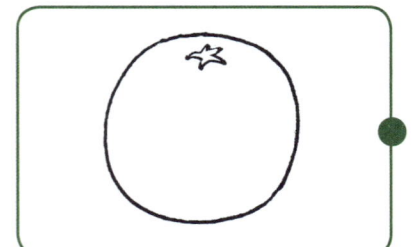

Sally 1 Activity Book © 2015 Cornelsen Schulverlage GmbH, Berlin

1   Listen and number.

1 ✏️ Count and write.

2 💬 Tell.

1 👂 ✏️ Listen and number.

☐

☐

☐

☐

2 💬 Tell.

Sally 1 Activity Book © 2015 Cornelsen Schulverlage GmbH, Berlin

CD 2.8   **29**

1 🖊 Circle.

2 💬 Tell.

Sally 1 Activity Book © 2015 Cornelsen Schulverlage GmbH, Berlin

1  Draw or stick in.

2 💬 Tell.

Sally 1 Activity Book © 2015 Cornelsen Schulverlage GmbH, Berlin

Goldilocks and the three bears

1 👂👉 Listen and point.　　**2** 👂🖌 Listen and colour.

Sally 1 Activity Book © 2015 Oldenbourg Schulbuchverlag

3 💬 Act out the story.

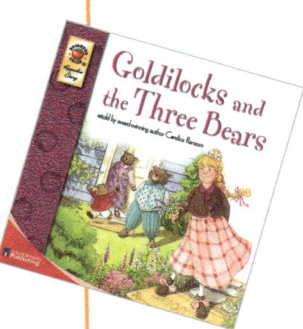

Merry Christmas

1 👂👉 Listen and point.

2 🖌 Colour.

Salty 1 Activity Book © 2015 Cornelsen Schulverlage GmbH, Berlin

3 💬 Tell.

1 Make your own wish list.
Draw or stick in. Present.

1 👂 🖌 Listen and draw.

Sally 1 Activity Book © 2015 Cornelsen Schulverlage GmbH, Berlin

1  Colour.

2 💬 Tell.

Happy birthday

1 Listen and point.

2 Count and write.

3 Colour.

  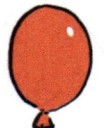    

4 Tell.

Sally 1 Activity Book © 2015 Cornelsen Schulverlage GmbH, Berlin

1   Play the game in your group.

2

1

3

8

4

7

5

9

2

1

3

8

4

7

5

6